Benchmark Assessment

Bothell, WA • Chicago, IL • Columbus, OH • New York, NY

Send all inquiries to:
McGraw-Hill Education
Two Penn Plaza
New York, New York 10121

Printed in the United States of America

6 7 8 9 RHR 17 16 15
C

The McGraw·Hill Companies

Table of Contents

Benchmark Assessment

Benchmark Assessment is an integral part of the complete assessment program aligned with ***McGraw-Hill Reading Wonders*** and the Common Core State Standards (CCSS).

Purpose of *Benchmark Assessment*

Benchmark Assessment reports on the outcome of your children's learning. The results of ***Benchmark Assessment*** serve as a summative assessment by providing a way to measure children's progress through the CCSS-aligned curriculum. The results of the assessments can be used to inform subsequent instruction, aid in making leveling and grouping decisions, and point toward areas in need of reteaching or remediation.

Benchmark Assessment tests provide students valuable practice in preparing for the type of high-stakes testing they will begin to encounter as they progress through school.

Focus of *Benchmark Assessment*

Benchmark Assessment focuses on key areas of English Language Arts as identified by the CCSS: comprehension of literature and informational text, phonics and decoding skills, and recognition of high-frequency words.

Administering *Benchmark Assessment*

Benchmark Test 1 should be administered mid-year, after instruction for Units 1–5 has been completed. Benchmark Test 2 should be administered close to the end of the year. Teacher script, including the comprehension selections and all test items, precedes the Answer Key for each test.

Make copies of the benchmark assessment for the class. You will need one copy of the Answer Key page that features the scoring table for each child taking the assessment. This table provides a place to list children's scores. The data from each benchmark assessment charts children's progress and underscores strengths and weaknesses.

After each child has a copy of the assessment, provide a version of the following directions: **Say:** *Write your name and the date on the top of each page of this test.* (When children are finished, continue with the directions.) *I will read four stories aloud. I also will read questions. Some of the questions will be about the stories. Some of the questions will ask you about sounds or words. Draw a circle around the correct answer for each question. When we have completed the test, put your pencil down and turn the pages over. We will begin now.*

Answer procedural questions during the assessment. After the class has completed the assessment, ask children to verify that their names and the date are written on the necessary pages.

Overview of *Benchmark Assessment*

Benchmark Assessment consists of two tests. Benchmark Test 1 focuses on skills taught in Units 1–5; Benchmark Test 2 samples skills from the entire year.

Each benchmark assessment is composed of the following:

- 4 comprehension selections
- 1 sample item
- 10 items assessing Comprehension Skills
- 10 items assessing Phonics
- 5 items assessing High-Frequency Words

Comprehension Selections and Items

Each benchmark assessment features four comprehension selections for you to read aloud to the children. Two selections are fiction, two are informational. Comprehension items in each test assess your children's understanding of the text by use of Comprehension Skills.

Reading Foundations Items

Each benchmark assessment also includes items that assess your children's phonics skills and their ability to recognize high-frequency words. See the list above for the number of items of each type that are included in the assessments.

Evaluating *Benchmark Assessment* Scores

Each item on the benchmark assessment is worth one point, for a total of twenty-five points per test.

The goal of each benchmark assessment is to evaluate children's mastery of previously-taught material and to gauge progress toward year-end goals. The expectation is for children to score 80% or higher on the assessment as a whole. For children who would benefit from additional instruction, assign appropriate lessons from the Tier 2 online PDFs. Use children's results in particular skill categories to guide your assignments.

The Answer Keys in ***Benchmark Assessment*** provide the information you need to understand your children's performance and plan for their individualized instructional and intervention needs.

This column lists the instructional content from the unit that is assessed in each item.

Item	Answer	Content Focus	CCSS	Complexity

This column lists the CCSS alignment for each assessment item.

This column lists the Depth of Knowledge associated with each item.

10	boil the sap	Key Details	RI.K.1	DOK 1
11	soap	Initial *s*	RF.K.3a	DOK 1

Comprehension 1, 2, 3, 4, 5, 6, 7, 8, 9, 10	/10	%
Phonics 11, 12, 13, 14, 15, 16, 17, 18, 19, 20	/10	%

Scoring rows identify items by assessment focus and item type and allow for quick record keeping.

Name: ______________________ **Date:** ________

S

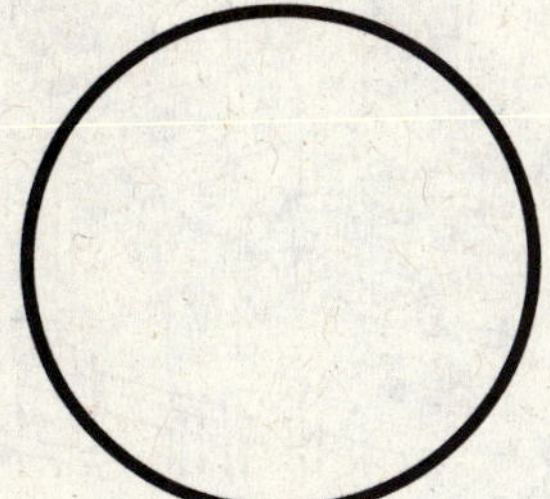

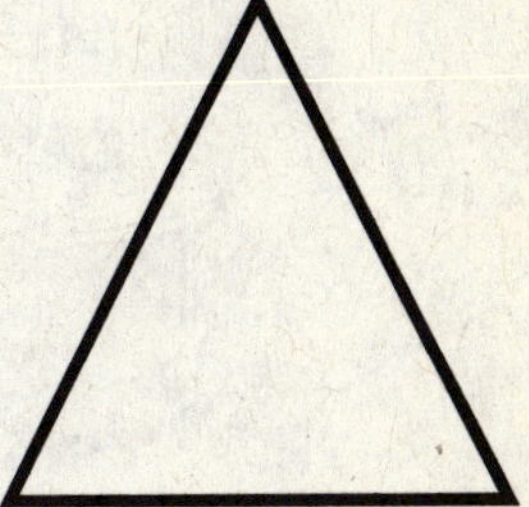

1

2

GO ON →

Name: ______________________ Date: __________

3

4

5

GO ON →

Name: ______________________ Date: __________

6

7

GO ON →

Name: ______________________ Date: ________

8

9

10

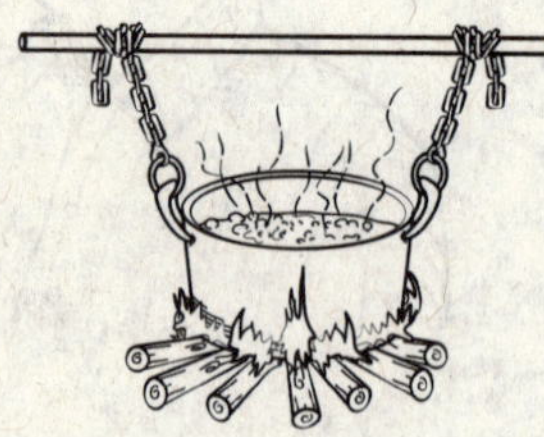

GO ON →

Name: ______________________________ Date: __________

s

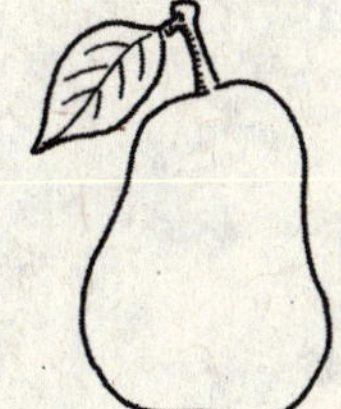

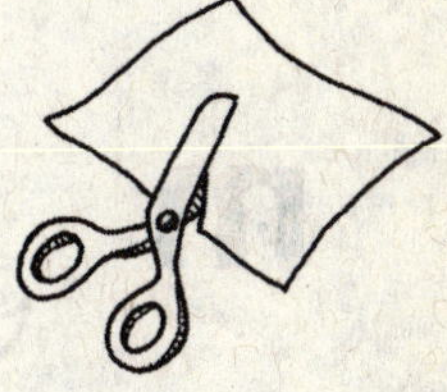

12

h

13

f

GO ON →

Name: ______________________ **Date:** __________

14

m   

15

p  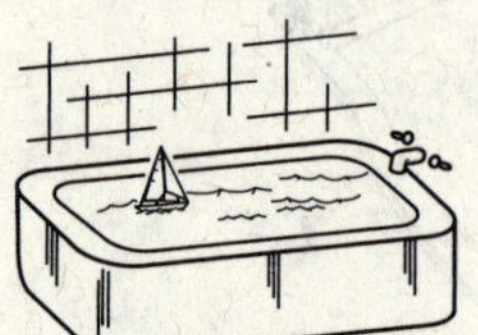 

16

t  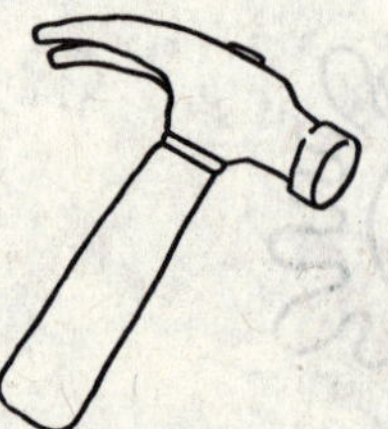 

GO ON →

Name: ______________________ Date: __________

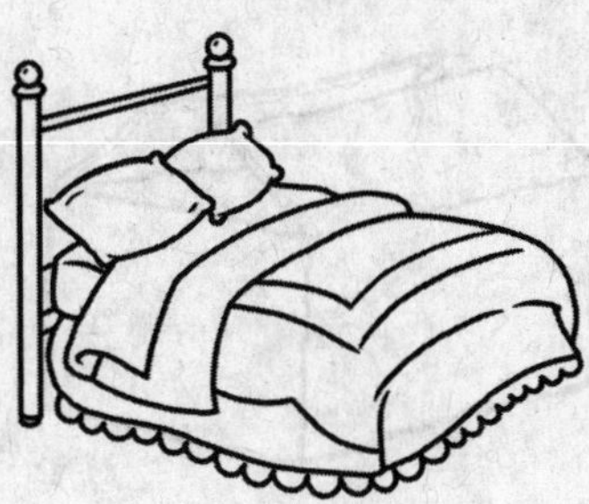

man **mat** **mad**

18

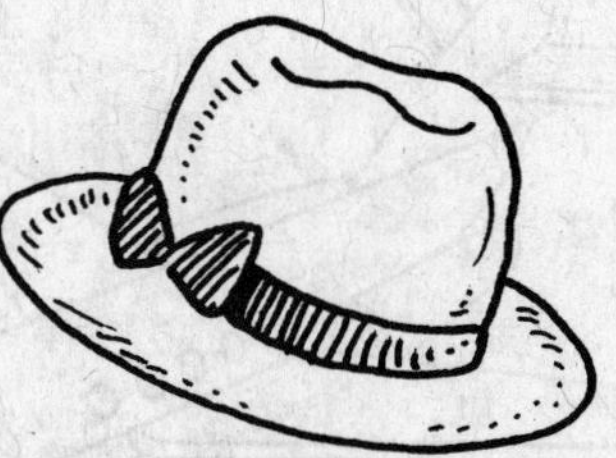

not **nap** **net**

GO ON →

Name: ______________________ Date: __________

19

pat pet pot

20

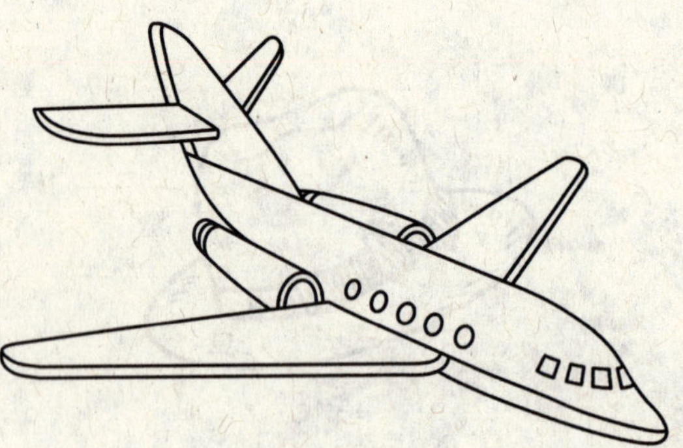

red ran rod

GO ON →

Name: ______________________ Date: __________

21

do my are

22

see like can

23

we the to

GO ON →

Name: ______________________ Date: __________

24

I and go

25

with he you

STOP

Grade K Benchmark Assessment 1 Teacher Script

Teacher reads all directions, passages, items, and answer choices aloud.

Comprehension

You are going to hear a story. After I read the story, I will ask you some questions. Listen carefully. We will begin now.

Cute Little Bugs

Have you ever seen a ladybug? Ladybugs are cute little bugs. They are almost round. Most ladybugs are red or orange with black spots.

Farmers like ladybugs. Ladybugs eat other bugs. These other bugs are pests. They kill the plants that farmers grow. So the ladybugs help farmers.

In the winter, ladybugs sometimes go inside houses. You may find them on a wall or window. They do not hurt people or houses. But you may want them to stay outside.

Turn to the first page.
Check to see that all the children are on the correct page.

Point to the row of pictures where you see the letter S.
Hold up page 1, pointing to the S for children to see.

I will read a question. Listen to the question as I read it aloud: What shape are ladybugs? Look at the three pictures in the row. Choose the picture that shows the answer to the question and draw a circle around it. What is the answer?
Have a child provide the answer.

Yes, the first picture shows a round shape. The story says that ladybugs are almost round.
Check to see that children have circled the correct picture.

Does anyone have any questions?

Now I will read the story again. Listen carefully.
Read the story aloud again.

Now point to the row of pictures next to the number 1.
Check to see that all the children are at the correct place.

Now I'm going to read two more questions. Listen to each question as I read it aloud.

1. *What is this story mostly about? Look at the pictures. Draw a circle around the picture that shows what the story is mostly about.*
2. *Point to number 2. Look at the pictures. Which picture shows who gets help from ladybugs? Draw a circle around the picture that shows who gets help from ladybugs.*

Turn to page 2.

Check to see that all the children are on the correct page.

Now I will read another story. Then I will ask you some more questions. Listen carefully.

Ben's New Friend

Ben loved free time at school. His favorite thing to do was play with blocks.

One day a new girl came to Ben's class. The teacher said the girl's name was Molly. At free time, Molly started playing with the blocks. Ben was upset.

Ben tried making a ball out of clay. He tried drawing with crayons. Then he went over and stood next to Molly.

"Do you want to help me build a castle with blocks?" asked Molly.

"Yes!" said Ben. He sat down next to Molly and picked up a block.

3 *Point to number 3. Look at the three pictures about the story. Where does this story take place? Draw a circle around the picture that shows where the story takes place.*

4 *Point to number 4. Look at the three pictures about the story. Who gets upset? Draw a circle around the picture that shows who gets upset.*

5 *Point to number 5. Look at the pictures. What does Ben do last? Draw a circle around the picture that shows what Ben does last.*

Turn to page 3.

Check to see that all the children are on the correct page.

Now I will read another story. Then I will ask you some more questions. Listen carefully.

Meena's Neighborhood

Meena and her dad were walking in the neighborhood. They saw some newspapers and food wrappers on the ground. This trash made the neighborhood look ugly.

Dad got an idea. He invited the neighbors to a clean-up day. People got trash bags and work gloves. They picked up all of the trash. The neighborhood looked beautiful!

At the end of the day, the neighbors had a picnic in the park. Everyone brought tasty food and had a good time.

6 *Point to number 6. What is this story mostly about? Draw a circle around the picture that shows what this story is mostly about.*

7 *Point to number 7. Look at the pictures. Who has the idea to clean up? Draw a circle around the picture that shows who has the idea to clean up.*

Turn to page 4.

Check to see that all the children are on the correct page.

Now I will read another story. Then I will ask you some more questions. Listen carefully.

Food from a Tree

Most farmers grow food in the ground. But some farmers get a special food from a kind of tree. This food is maple syrup!

Maple syrup comes from the sap, or juice, in maple trees. At the end of winter, farmers make holes in the trees. The sap drips out. Farmers collect the sap in buckets.

Then farmers turn the sap into syrup. They boil the sap until it gets thick and sweet. They pour it into bottles and jugs. Last, they sell it to people who put it on their pancakes!

8 *Point to number 8. Look at the pictures. What is this story mostly about? Draw a circle around the picture that shows what the story is about.*

9 *Point to number 9. Look at the pictures. Where does maple syrup come from? Draw a circle around the picture that shows where the syrup comes from.*

10 *Point to number 10. Look at the pictures. What do farmers do with the sap after they collect it? Draw a circle around the picture that shows what farmers do with the sap after they collect it.*

Phonics

Turn to page 5.

Check to see that all the children are on the correct page.

Point to number 11.

Check to see that all the children are at the correct place.

11 *Look at the letter* s. *What sound does it make? Listen to the names of the pictures:* soap, pear, cut. *Draw a circle around the picture whose name begins with the /s/ sound.*

12 *Point to number 12. Look at the letter* h. *What sound does it make? Listen to the names of the pictures:* rug, horse, fan. *Draw a circle around the picture whose name begins with the /h/ sound.*

13 *Point to number 13. Look at the letter* f. *What sound does it make? Listen to the names of the pictures:* sun, fish, cap. *Draw a circle around the picture whose name begins with the /f/ sound.*

Turn to page 6.

Check to see that all the children are on the correct page.

14 *Point to number 14. Look at the letter* m. *What sound does it make? Listen to the names of the pictures:* moon, coat, broom. *Circle the picture whose name ends with the /m/ sound.*

15 *Point to number 15. Look at the letter* p. *What sound does it make? Listen to the names of the pictures:* pan, tub, map. *Draw a circle around the picture whose name ends with the /p/ sound.*

16 *Point to number 16. Look at the letter* t. *What sound does it make? Listen to the names of the pictures:* knot, tool, door. *Draw a circle around the picture whose name ends with the /t/ sound.*

Turn to page 7.

Check to see that all the children are on the correct page.

17 *Point to number 17. Look at the picture of the bed. Listen to the ending sound in* bed. *Now read the words. Draw a circle around the word that has the same ending sound as* bed.

18 *Point to number 18. Look at the picture of the hat. Listen to the middle sound in* hat. *Now read the words. Draw a circle around the word that has the same middle sound as* hat.

Turn to page 8.

Check to see that all the children are on the correct page.

19 *Point to number 19. Look at the picture of the box. Listen to the middle sound in* box. *Now read the words. Draw a circle around the word that has the same middle sound as* box.

20 *Point to number 20. Look at the picture of the jet. Listen to the middle sound in* jet. *Now read the words. Draw a circle around the word that has the same middle sound as* jet.

High-Frequency Words

Turn to page 9.

Check to see that all the children are on the correct page.

Point to number 21.

Check to see that all the children are at the correct place.

21 *Look at the words. Find the word* do. *She will* do *that. Draw a circle around the word* do.

22 *Point to number 22. Look at the words. Find the word* can. *They* can *swim. Draw a circle around the word* can.

23 *Point to number 23. Look at the words. Find the word* the. *Where is* the *game? Draw a circle around the word* the.

Turn to page 10.

Check to see that all the children are on the correct page.

Point to number 24.

Check to see that all the children are at the correct place.

24 *Look at the words. Find the word* and. *They have a cat* and *a dog. Draw a circle around the word* and.

25 *Point to number 25. Look at the words. Find the word* you. *Where are* you*? Draw a circle around the word* you.

Answer Key

Name: ______________________

Item	Answer	Content Focus	CCSS	Complexity
1	ladybug	Main Topic and Key Details	RI.K.2	DOK 2
2	farmer	Key Details	RI.K.7	DOK 1
3	classroom	Character, Setting, Events	RL.K.3	DOK 1
4	boy (Ben)	Character, Setting, Events	RL.K.3	DOK 1
5	picking up block	Key Details	RL.K.1	DOK 1
6	people filling trash bags	Main Topic and Key Details	RL.K.2	DOK 2
7	man (Meena's dad)	Main Topic and Key Details	RL.K.2	DOK 1
8	maple syrup	Main Topic and Key Details	RI.K.2	DOK 2
9	maple tree	Main Topic and Key Details	RI.K.2	DOK 1
10	boil the sap	Key Details	RI.K.1	DOK 1
11	soap	Initial *s*	RF.K.3a	DOK 1
12	horse	Initial *h*	RF.K.3a	DOK 1
13	fish	Initial *f*	RF.K.3a	DOK 1
14	broom	Final *m*	RF.K.3a	DOK 1
15	map	Final *p*	RF.K.3a	DOK 1
16	knot	Final *t*	RF.K.3a	DOK 1
17	mad	Final *d*	RF.K.3a	DOK 1
18	nap	Medial *a*	RF.K.3b	DOK 1
19	pot	Medial *o*	RF.K.3b	DOK 1
20	red	Medial *e*	RF.K.3b	DOK 1

Answer Key

Name: ____________________

Item	Answer	Content Focus	CCSS	Complexity
21	do	High-Frequency Words	RF.K.3c	DOK 1
22	can	High-Frequency Words	RF.K.3c	DOK 1
23	the	High-Frequency Words	RF.K.3c	DOK 1
24	and	High-Frequency Words	RF.K.3c	DOK 1
25	you	High-Frequency Words	RF.K.3c	DOK 1

Comprehension 1, 2, 3, 4, 5, 6, 7, 8, 9, 10	/10	%
Phonics 11, 12, 13, 14, 15, 16, 17, 18, 19, 20	/10	%
High-Frequency Words 21, 22, 23, 24, 25	/5	%
Total Benchmark Assessment Score	/25	%

Name: ______________________ **Date:** __________

S

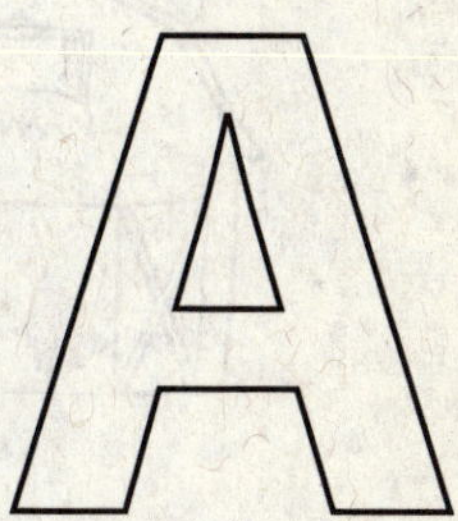

1

2

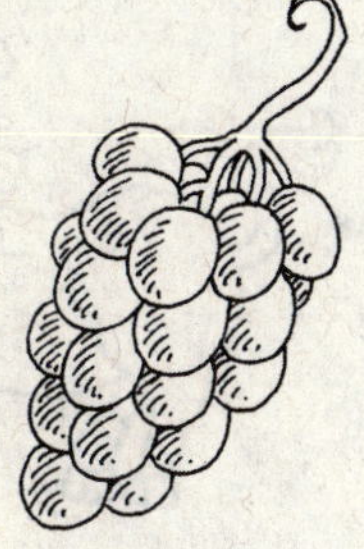
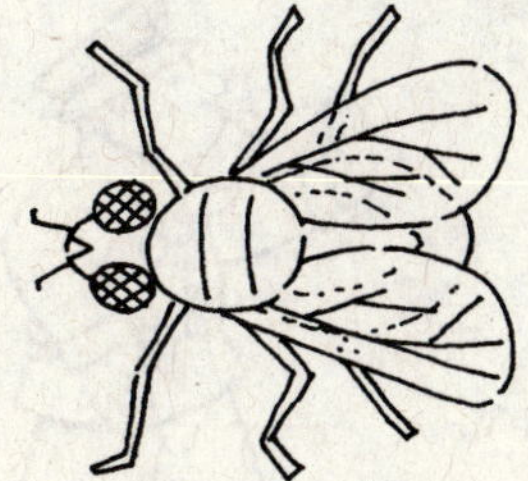

GO ON →

Name: ______________________ Date: ________

3

4

5

GO ON →

Name: ______________________ **Date:** ________

6

7

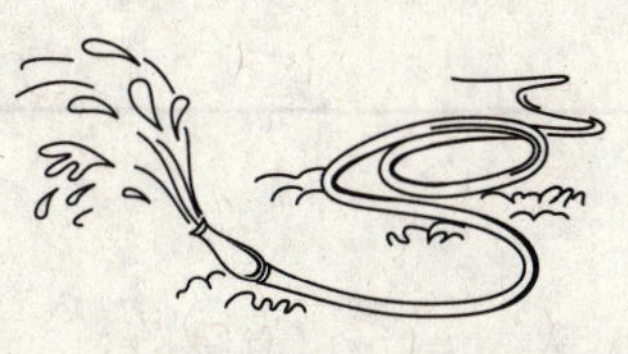

8

GO ON →

Name: ______________________ Date: __________

9

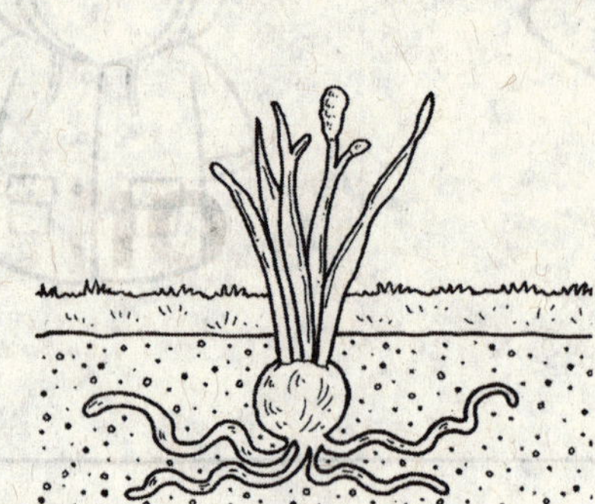

10

GO ON →

Name: ______________________ Date: __________

11

lone zone cat

12

yet vet wet

13

jog got quit

GO ON →

Name: ______________________ Date: __________

14

rat rag bed

15

sat sip rock

16

fit six fin

GO ON →

Name: ______________________ **Date:** __________

17

pig **hot** **nut**

18

peg **lug** **bad**

GO ON →

Name: ______________________________ Date: __________

role **ripe** **rap**

20

kit **cot** **like**

GO ON →

Name: ______________________ Date: __________

21

they this good

22

where want are

23

there look little

GO ON →

Name: ______________________________ Date: ________

24

have help play

25

does do was

STOP

Grade K Benchmark Assessment 2 Teacher Script

Teacher reads all directions, passages, items, and answer choices aloud.

Comprehension

You are going to hear a story. After I read the story, I will ask you some questions. Listen carefully. We will begin now.

Welcoming Spring

Peep! Peep! Peep! When you hear this loud sound at night, you know that spring has arrived. "Peep, peep, peep" is the noise that the spring peeper makes.

The spring peeper is a tree frog. It looks a lot like the frogs you see in ponds. But it's very small and either gray or brown. It's a little longer than a paper clip. It has a dark mark on its back that looks like the letter X.

The spring peeper lives near trees. It also needs a place with water. It likes swamps, ponds, and other wet places.

The spring peeper eats bugs like flies and spiders. It hides during the day so that a bird or other animal won't eat it!

Turn to the first page.
Check to see that all the children are on the correct page.

Point to the row of pictures where you see the letter S.
Hold up page 1, pointing to the *S* for children to see.

I will read a question. Listen to the question as I read it aloud: What letter shape is on the back of a spring peeper? Look at the three letter pictures in the row: W, X, A. *Choose the picture that shows the answer to the question and draw a circle around it. What is the answer?*
Have a child provide the answer.

Yes, the second picture shows the letter X. *The story says that the spring peeper has a mark on its back in the shape of an* X.
Check to see that children have circled the correct picture.

Does anyone have any questions?

Now I will read the story again. Listen carefully.
Read the story aloud again.

Now point to the row of pictures next to the number 1.
Check to see that all the children are at the correct place.

Now I'm going to read two more questions. Listen to each question as I read it aloud.

1. *What is this story mostly about? Look at the pictures. Draw a circle around the picture that shows what the story is mostly about.*

2. *Point to number 2. What do spring peepers eat? Look at the pictures. Draw a circle around the picture that shows what spring peepers eat.*

Turn to page 2.

Check to see that all the children are on the correct page.

Now I will read another story. Then I will ask you some more questions. Listen carefully.

The Seeds That Wouldn't Grow

Bernie the Bird loved to sing. Bernie sang so well that a farmer gave him a birdhouse. Even the cats in the barnyard loved to hear him sing.

Bernie wanted a flower garden. So he got some seeds. He put the seeds in his birdhouse and sang to them. The seeds didn't grow. So Bernie sang louder. Still, the seeds did nothing.

A farmer heard Bernie singing. She said, "Plant those seeds in the ground to make them grow. You must water them, too."

So that's what Bernie did. Soon the plants began to grow. Then Bernie sang to the plants. They seemed to like it.

3 *Point to number 3. Look at the pictures. Bernie the Bird has a problem. What does he want? Draw a circle around the picture that shows what Bernie wants.*

4 *Point to number 4. Look at the pictures. When Bernie wants his seeds to grow, what does he do first? Draw a circle around the picture that shows what Bernie does first.*

5 *Point to number 5. Look at the pictures. Who helps Bernie solve his problem? Draw a circle around the picture that shows who helps Bernie.*

Turn to page 3.

Check to see that all the children are on the correct page.

Now I will read another story. Then I will ask you some more questions. Listen carefully.

Hannah's Galoshes

Hannah loved her new galoshes. They had red flowers and butterflies on them. They kept her feet nice and dry.

On Monday, Hannah wanted to wear the galoshes to school, but she couldn't. The day was sunny and warm. Tuesday, Wednesday, and Thursday were the same. Every morning she woke up to a sunny sky.

Thursday night it rained all night long. The next morning Hannah looked out the window, but it was sunny again. "No galoshes today either," she thought.

It was time to go to school. After breakfast, her mom said, "Don't forget your galoshes! It's wet and muddy out there."

So Hannah wore her galoshes to school!

6 *Point to number 6. Look at the pictures. Which picture shows what Hannah should wear to keep her feet nice and dry? Draw a circle around the picture that shows what Hannah should wear to keep her feet dry.*

7 *Point to number 7. Look at the pictures. Why does Hannah's mom tell her to wear her galoshes on Friday morning? Draw a circle around the picture that shows why Hannah's mom wants her to wear her galoshes on Friday.*

8 *Point to number 8. Look at the pictures. Where does Hannah go at the very end of the story? Draw a circle around the picture that shows where Hannah goes at the end of the story.*

Turn to page 4.
Check to see that all the children are on the correct page.

Now I will read another story. Then I will ask you some more questions. Listen carefully.

Spring Daffodils

Flowers grow in different ways. Roses grow on bushes. Sunflowers and daisies grow from seeds. Some flowers, like daffodils and tulips, grow from bulbs. Daffodils are pretty yellow flowers you see in early spring.

A daffodil bulb is a round ball that holds the flower's food. You plant the bulb in the fall. The bulb sends out roots to gather water. In the spring, the soil warms up. The roots take in more water. The plant begins to grow.

The plant uses the food in the bulb, and the leaves begin to grow. They grow straight up toward the sunlight. Soon, the leaves and stem of the flower break through the soil. The daffodil plant grows taller. Then, a yellow flower blooms! It lasts only a few days before it droops.

9 *Point to number 9. Look at the pictures. What happens to the daffodil bulb right after the soil warms in the spring? Draw a circle around the picture that shows what happens to the daffodil bulb right after the soil warms in the spring.*

10 *Point to number 10. Look at the pictures of a rose, a daisy, and a tulip. The story says that one of these flowers is like a daffodil because it grows from a bulb. Which kind of flower grows from a bulb? Is it a rose, a daisy, or a tulip? Draw a circle around the picture of the flower that is like a daffodil because it grows from a bulb.*

Phonics

Turn to page 5.

Check to see that all the children are on the correct page.

Point to number 11.

Check to see that all the children are at the correct place.

11 *Look at the picture of a cone. Listen to the beginning sound in* cone. *Now read the words. Draw a circle around the word that has the same beginning sound as* cone.

12 *Point to number 12. Look at the picture of a van. Listen to the beginning sound in* van. *Now read the words. Draw a circle around the word that has the same beginning sound as* van.

13 *Point to number 13. Look at the picture of a man doing a job. Listen to the beginning sound in* job. *Now read the words. Draw a circle around the word that has the same beginning sound as* job.

Turn to page 6.

Check to see that all the children are on the correct page.

Point to number 14.

Check to see that all the children are at the correct place.

14 *Look at the picture of a bug. Listen to the ending sound in* bug. *Now read the words. Draw a circle around the word that has the same ending sound as* bug.

15 *Point to number 15. Look at the picture of a dock. Listen to the ending sound in* dock. *Now read the words. Draw a circle around the word that has the same ending sound as* dock.

16 *Point to number 16. Look at the picture that shows how to fix a tire. Listen to the ending sound in* fix. *Now read the words. Draw a circle around the word that has the same ending sound as* fix.

Turn to page 7.

Check to see that all the children are on the correct page.

Point to number 17.

Check to see that all the children are at the correct place.

17 *Look at the picture of a hut. Listen to the vowel sound in* hut. *Now read the words. Draw a circle around the word that has the same vowel sound as* hut.

18 *Look at the picture of a leg. Listen to the vowel sound in* leg. *Now read the words. Draw a circle around the word that has the same vowel sound as* leg.

Turn to page 8.

Check to see that all the children are on the correct page.

Point to number 19.

Check to see that all the children are at the correct place.

19 *Look at the picture of a rope. Listen to the vowel sound in* rope. *Now read the words. Draw a circle around the word that has the same vowel sound as* rope.

20 *Point to number 20. Look at the picture of a kite. Listen to the vowel sound in* kite. *Now read the words. Draw a circle around the word that has the same vowel sound as* kite.

High-Frequency Words

Turn to page 9.

Check to see that all the children are on the correct page.

Point to number 21.

Check to see that all the children are at the correct place.

21 *Look at the words. Find the word* this. This *is my book. Draw a circle around the word* this.

22 *Point to number 22. Look at the words. Find the word* where. Where *is my backpack? Draw a circle around the word* where.

23 *Point to number 23. Look at the words. Find the word* little. *The frog is* little. *Draw a circle around the word* little.

Turn to page 10.

Check to see that all the children are on the correct page.

Point to number 24.

Check to see that all the children are at the correct place.

24 *Look at the words. Find the word* help. *I* help *Dad rake the leaves. Draw a circle around the word* help.

25 *Point to number 25. Find the word* does. *What* does *the sign say? Draw a circle around the word* does.

Answer Key Name: ______________________

Item	Answer	Content Focus	CCSS	Complexity
1	frog	Main Topic and Key Details	RI.K.2	DOK 2
2	fly	Key Details	RI.K.1	DOK 1
3	garden	Plot: Problem and Solution	RL.K.3	DOK 2
4	bird singing	Plot: Sequence	RL.K.3	DOK 1
5	farmer	Plot: Problem and Solution	RL.K.3	DOK 2
6	galoshes	Key Details: Use Illustrations	RL.K.7	DOK 1
7	mud puddle	Plot: Cause and Effect	RL.K.3	DOK 2
8	school	Character, Setting, Events	RL.K.3	DOK 1
9	daffodil growing	Connections Within Text: Sequence	RI.K.3	DOK 1
10	tulip	Connections Within Text: Compare and Contrast	RI.K.3	DOK 2
11	cat	Initial *c*	RF.K.3a	DOK 1
12	vet	Initial *v*	RF.K.3a	DOK 1
13	jog	Initial *j*	RF.K.3a	DOK 1
14	rag	Final *g*	RF.K.3a	DOK 1
15	rock	Final *ck*	RF.1.3a	DOK 1
16	six	Final *x*	RF.K.3a	DOK 1
17	nut	Short *u*	RF.K.3b	DOK 1
18	peg	Short *e*	RF.K.3b	DOK 1
19	role	Long *o* (*o_e*, *o*)	RF.K.3b	DOK 1
20	like	Long *i* (*i_e*)	RF.K.3b	DOK 1

Answer Key Name: ______________________________

Item	Answer	Content Focus	CCSS	Complexity
21	this	High-Frequency Words	RF.K.3c	DOK 1
22	where	High-Frequency Words	RF.K.3c	DOK 1
23	little	High-Frequency Words	RF.K.3c	DOK 1
24	help	High-Frequency Words	RF.K.3c	DOK 1
25	does	High-Frequency Words	RF.K.3c	DOK 1

Comprehension 1, 2, 3, 4, 5, 6, 7, 8, 9, 10	/10	%
Phonics 11, 12, 13, 14, 15, 16, 17, 18, 19, 20	/10	%
High-Frequency Words 21, 22, 23, 24, 25	/5	%
Total Benchmark Assessment Score	/25	%